"Neither scale nor perseverance has anything to do with success in art, and Mr. Dinnerstein's triptych could be just one more painstaking failure. But it succeeds as an echo chamber, as a scrupulous representation of a suburb in the sticks, as a portrait of young people who are trying to make an honorable go of life and as an inventory of the kind of thing that in 1975 give such people a sense of their own identity. Today is the last day of the show, but the triptych will be available to interested persons until further notice. It deserves to go to a museum."

John Russell, Senior Art Critic,
The New York Times, February 5, 1975

"This little-known masterpiece of 1970s realism was begun by the young Simon Dinnerstein during a Fulbright Fellowship in Germany and completed in his hometown, Brooklyn, three years later. Incorporating carefully rendered art postcards, children's drawings and personal memorabilia; a formidable worktable laid out with printmaking tools and outdoor views; and the artist and his family, it synthesizes portrait, still life, interior and landscape and rummages through visual culture while sampling a dazzling range of textures and representational styles. It should be seen by anyone interested in the history of recent art and its oversights."

Roberta Smith, Senior Art Critic,
The New York Times, August 11, 2011

1. The Fulbright Triptych 1971-74
oil on wood panels, 14 feet in width, framed and separated

The Fulbright Triptych

"No one could accuse Simon Dinnerstein of being a fashionable artist. Not at the time he began, not know, and not at any time in between. Leafing through the catalog of his mature work that now spans four decades, one is struck immediately by his total disregard for prevailing taste; his apparent disinterest in the visual arguments of advanced art circles, and conversely by his single-minded concentration upon the development of a highly personal, creative pursuit."

— Thomas M. Messer, Director Emeritus, Guggenheim Museum

"Simon Dinnerstein's art evokes, for me, something reminiscent of Marcel Proust in which memories of the past, the actual present, and dreams of the future are curiously interchangeable. I love his sense of "time suspension", suggesting that all earlier times may co-exist with the present time. I guess I'm trying to do something similar in my composition!

Dinnerstein's work is very spiritual and haunting. At the same time it reflects the beauty of our physical existence. I do get a strong sense of the fragility of life in his work, very much like François Villon's "Where are the snows of yesteryear?"

— George Crumb, composer, *Ancient Voices of Children*

"Simon Dinnerstein paints with a reverence for life that is rare. The radiance of his light can transform reality into a presence that is essential, mythic and dreamlike."

— George Tooker, artist, *The Subway, Government Bureau*

"In *The Fulbright Triptych* Dinnerstein continues the life of 'A.' Being an artist, yet also recognizing oneself as the protagonist in an artist's project, must evoke curious and complex feelings – not unlike seeing oneself turn or being turned into a character in a novel."

— J.M. Coetzee, author, *Disgrace*

"The people at the German consulate believe so fiercely in *The Fulbright Triptych* that, after the Dinnerstein exhibition closes, the painting will remain in place, in the consulate's lobby. The Met should try to carve out a slot in its exhibition schedule during this period and persuade all concerned to let it give the triptych a small, properly professional show, possibly with some of the large charcoal portrait drawings that Mr. Dinnerstein made during the same period. The four examples reproduced in the book about the triptych look fabulous. Because ultimately the single most startling fact about Mr. Dinnerstein's *Fulbright Triptych* is that it has never had the honor — which it richly deserves — of being exhibited in a major museum, in New York or anywhere else. If it were, anyone interested in the history of recent art and its oversights would be beyond lucky."

— Roberta Smith, Senior Art Critic, *The New York Times*

"I must think and think again about the *Triptych*. Obviously you have put everything into it. My immediate feeling about it – and practically all your work— is that it is a perfect register (narrative, if you will, art-as-equivalent-at-the-highest-articulateness) of the Jewish soul. Fred Siegel once gave me a poster from a school. It is a lesson in the letter aleph, showing that the upper yod symbolizes Torah and God, the lower one is human life, and the diagonal is the boundary between the two. The illustration is of a family studying Torah at the kitchen (or dining room) table — father, mother, daughter, and son. The *Triptych* says something of the same thing— and lots more.

It is an iconographer's heaven! That's Germany – Germany!— out the windows. "Here we are, a family. We have been civilized for five thousand years. We have experienced everything; we have survived. We flourish." Images of Assyria and Babylon to the right; children's drawings— renewal— to the left.

Zukofsky's "A" in paint!"

— Guy Davenport, author, *The Geography of the Imagination*

"Simon Dinnerstein's *Fulbright Triptych* is one of those singular and astonishing works of art which seem to imply a description of the whole world merely by insisting on a scrupulous gaze at one perfect instant."

— Jonathan Lethem, author, *The Fortress of Solitude*

"Two windows, both in the painting's central panel, offer a bird's-eye view of the village, revealing a placid street and the rooftops of single-family homes. The "inventory" consists of postcards depicting works of art, mostly Northern Renaissance paintings, which hang on the wall alongside sketches suggesting works in progress. On the right panel is a self-portrait, and on the left panel a portrait of the artist's wife and daughter, also seated and frontal. The piece signals Dinnerstein's continuing interests: the figure, his family and friends, and old-master artists. Among the artists who have influenced him, he says, are van Eyck, Dürer, and Rembrandt, and the twentieth-century artists who emulate them, such as Andrew Wyeth and, perhaps unexpectedly, Edward Weston. There is always an air of moody insularity to Dinnerstein's works, as though the studio were a *hortus conclusus*, a sort of prelapsarian space signaling Dinnerstein's self-sufficiency."

— Donald Kuspit, Contributing Editor, *Art Forum*

"One of the first associations I had upon seeing your painting was with Agnès Varda's film *The Gleaners and I. The Fulbright Triptych* seems to me a culmination of a lifetime spent gleaning - be it objects, images, quotes, memories, or thoughts. I get the impression of someone for whom thinking, creating, and living one's life are all intimately intertwined. I presume that when you collected all of these things, you never intended to put them directly into a painting."

— Tim Nicholas, filmmaker, writer

"My father's *Triptych* has loomed large in my life. It tells the story of my parents right before I was conceived, through my infancy. It's a story that I find endlessly fascinating. Who were they then?

So the *Triptych* was born at the same time as I was, and it contains my parents' DNA just as much as I do. When I look at the *Triptych* I see where I come from. And if I wanted to tell someone who I really am deep inside, I would just need to show them those three panels.

— Simone Dinnerstein, pianist

THE LASTING WORLD

SIMON DINNERSTEIN

AND THE FULBRIGHT TRIPTYCH

THE LASTING WORLD

SIMON DINNERSTEIN

AND THE FULBRIGHT TRIPTYCH

First Street Editions

THE LASTING WORLD: SIMON DINNERSTEIN AND THE FULBRIGHT TRIPTYCH

This catalog accompanies the exhibit *The Lasting World: Simon Dinnerstein and The Fulbright Triptych.*

Exhibition Dates

Museum of Art and Archeology, University of Missouri - Columbia, July 28 - Dec 24, 2017

Arnot Art Museum, Elmira, New York, March 9 - June 30, 2018

Nevada Museum of Art, Reno, Nevada,   July 21, 2018 - January 7, 2019

Published by First Street Editions

First Street Editions, 415 First Street, Brooklyn, New York 11215

The text of this book is set in Minion.

Printed in China through Four Colour Print Group.

ISBN   978-0-692-87448-6

Front cover: *The Sink*, 1974

Back Cover: *Marie Bilderl*, 1971

Frontispiece 1: *The Fulbright Triptych*, 1971-1974 detail

Frontispiece 2: *Rear Window*, 1994 detail

Front flap: *The Fulbright Triptych*, 1971-1974 detail

Back flap: *The Fulbright Triptych*, 1971-1974 detail

Funding for this exhibition and catalog is made possible though the generous support of

Peter Scotese, New York

Museum of Art and Archaeology, University of Missouri-Columbia

Arnot Art Museum, Elmira, New York

Nevada Museum of Art, Reno, Nevada

Contents

Rudolf Arnheim

How do we recover the fugitive flight of time? Memory does its best. It recalls the cool spring, twenty years ago at the American Academy in Rome, where a group of fellows and residents had the chance to spend some time in the spirit of the Eternal City.

Among the artists in 1978 was Simon Dinnerstein. In his spacious studio I remember a large wall occupied by a faithful depiction of the flower market on the Campo dé Fiori. The painting reminded me compellingly also of the similar display at the foot of the Piazza di Spagna, where its symmetry, marked by the sales lady sitting in the center of the floral display, is in keeping with the overall symmetry of the Spanish Steps leading to the façade of the church of the Trinità dei Monti. This timelessness caught in the midst of a bustling city is in the character of Dinnerstein's work. It maintains the tradition of representing the lasting world as it lives in the work of the van Eycks, Dürer, Vermeer, and others.

Great paintings have always been more than a mere reflection of reality. But there is a particular quality I find in some of Dinnerstein's recent work. It is a kind of detachment from the immediacy of presence, an early example of what I find in Piero della Francesca's paintings. This quality has sometimes been called "magical realism." The figures are sharply outlined, which moves them from the realm of reality to that of depiction. There is a preference of frontality and profile, two firm positions resisting the natural turn of bodily movement in space.

Some of Dinnerstein's recent figures adopt these qualities of detachment because the naturalistic tradition has been affected by modern art. It has resisted the outer-worldliness of cubism as well as the plaster-cast puppets of make-believe. The influence of these stylistic developments remains noticeable, but Dinnerstein's independence preserves his endearing nearness to our world, even when he watches it with the detachment of the observer.

November 1998
Ann Arbor, Michigan

Rudolf Arnheim (1904-2007) was an art theorist and a professor of psychology. He was the author of *Art and Visual Perception, Entropy and Art* and *The Genesis of a Painting: Picasso's Guernica.*

2. The Kelton Press 1969

Alex Barker

I was first attracted to the work of Simon Dinnerstein by things that weren't there.

Perhaps I'm drawn to forms of expression that give the promise of understanding reality from the things it leaves in its wake. After all some of the things I'm most interested in as an archaeologist, like time, are never actually found but are instead inferred from other things. In my day job I try to understand a dynamic and fleeting world, full of life and ephemeral meaning, from the lasting world it leaves behind.

The exhibition title "The Lasting World" is from an essay on Simon's work by Rudolf Arnheim, an art theorist who once argued that images don't imitate reality, they hint at it. At first glance the realism of Simon's work seems to imitate reality, but instead it playfully confounds it, offering meaning less in what is seen than what is supposed.

Works like *The Sink* or *The Fulbright Triptych* are deceptive in their exactitude. Because of their painstaking realism they appear almost photographic, a passive representation of how light bounces off the objects in the picture plane. But ponder the works a bit more and their ambiguities—the fault lines along which they can be deconstructed—become more apparent.

In *The Sink*, for example, strongly-defined lines of perspective position the viewer in front of an alcove containing a small sink. A mirror above the sink reflects the room and part of a doorway, but curiously the artist (or the viewer, for that matter) does not appear in the mirror's reflection, even though the linear perspective emphasized by the doorway, walls, flooring and the sink itself all suggest he should. The image frames and points at a figure who is absent; we find the artist not in the image itself but in the ephemeral byproducts (brushes, roller, rags and cleaning supplies) of his work, by the things he left behind.

Consider *The Fulbright Triptych*. It seems straightforward enough—a moment in time during Simon's tenure as a Fulbright scholar studying printmaking in Germany, a triptych in which the tools of printmaking and the view through two windows occupy the central panel, while the artist, his wife and child occupy the wings. The walls are covered with postcards, mementos and works of inspiration or influence attached to pegboard, to all appearances what Jonathan Lethem called "a scrupulous gaze at one perfect instant."

But of course it's nothing of the sort. The square casement windows open onto a world that Simone, Simon's daughter—pictured on Renée's lap—could never have seen, as she was born after the couple returned to America. It's an imaginary time, set in a space that's equally imaginary for all its apparent verisimilitude. The main image and its flanking volets are parallel to the image plane, and all three images are depicted in rigorous one point perspective. Like *The Sink*, the one point perspective gives the scene a certain timelessness. But Simon, Renée and Simone upset this perspective, the young couple facing the viewer directly while the floorboards under their feet (floorboards based on those in a Brooklyn apartment, not the ostensible German scene depicted) sweep away at oblique angles toward that single point on the hidden horizon. The figures seem slightly out of place, temporary inhabitants of a space dominated by their tangible and timeless residue. Those figures look directly at us, but the layout of the scene focuses our gaze not immediately on them but on the point where all the other lines in the image converge. Like the figures, we know where that point must be but cannot see it, as it lies somewhere behind the ephemera tacked to the wall separating the two windows. Those ephemera define the figures at a moment in time, situating them in terms of family, friends, influences, and as the outcome of a series of constantly unfolding contingent events. They suggest the present as past-until-now, but also occlude the figures' view of that convergence point.

Throughout Simon's work there's loving attention to surfaces, from the paint splotches on mirrors to worn floorboards, from unflinching portrayals of skin—young and old—to exquisitely rendered gilt backdrops. While on the one hand they're real surfaces, real forms (one can play 'spot the shared details' between many otherwise unrelated works) they're used less as photorealistic backgrounds than to hint at the reality Simon seeks to capture. Those backgrounds, and the ephemera that populate his pictures, seem in some ways more lasting than the figures depicted. Figures seem fragile in their mortality and in their constant states of change, likely to vanish from view as does the unseen artist of *The Sink.* The solidity of figures is greatest when they parallel the picture plane, buttressed and supported by lines of perspective (*Arnold,* for example, or *Marie Bilderl*). In other works the figures seem cramped by the picture plane, trapped in a setting not of their choosing (e.g., *Renée*), passing through the picture plane rather than rooted in it, or overcoming its limitations in dreams.

In Simon's dream paintings we see a loosening of these constraints of space and linear time, as figures move through or over spaces that recede into nothingness. In his other works surroundings are defined—spaces and ephemera exist, so they're depicted in detail. Space and spatial juxtapositions become a way of hinting at time, at the constantly evolving lived experiences that cannot be easily captured in two dimensions. The images use their ostensible realism not to depict reality but to hint at it, to suggest the transient qualities of a temporal reality long in the past before the work of art it suggested can be completed, providing a narrative element that situates the figures as part of a story rather than a snapshot. That concern with time becomes clearer still when surveying the range of Simon's works. We see his family develop, watch stages of Renée's pregnancy and the growth of his daughter Simone, and later her own pregnancy and the growth of her family. That personal view of growth and change gives his works a poignancy that's as hard to describe as it is to evade.

Which brings us back to *The Fulbright Triptych*, to an apartment overlooking a small town in Germany, to a couple who violate the leading lines of the painting to confront the viewer. In the narrative, lasting world of the painting the figures remain forever young, forever looking back at us from a bricolage of ephemera and constructed space.

But in real life the young couple who gaze calmly back from the volets are now gone, replaced by their more mature selves further along a trajectory they could not see at the time, closer to a vanishing point in the distance obscured by their immediate surroundings, by the ephemera that remain.

Alex Barker is President-Elect, American Anthropological Association, Director, Museum of Art and Archaeology and Director, Museum of Anthropology at the University of Missouri.

3. Studio Still Life 1976

Tom Healy

Frank: Hey you wanna go for a ride?
Jeffrey: No thanks.
Frank: No thanks? What does that mean?
Jeffrey: I don't wanna go.
Frank: Go where?
Jeffrey: For a ride.
Frank: A ride! Hell that's a good idea!

— David Lynch, *Blue Velvet*

A door opens. Someone beckons. You hesitate. Do you get in?

Think of all the parables of encountering strangers. Foolishness and dread, fantasies of passion, sagas of empire, stories of love, fleeting friendships. They all follow brief and unstable first moments of thrill and fear. Why trust someone? Why not? We find ourselves out there on a knife-edge of unknowing. Maybe our lives will change forever.

We often say that something or someone catches or grabs our attention. Catch and grab. They're ancient words of hunting, chasing and setting traps. We're lured and taken in. We're prey. Maybe just as often, we're the ones hunting? Sometimes, we're just playing, operating on nothing more than what-the-hell. What do we choose? Or are we chosen?

Maybe I'm amping up the volume too much to talk about a first encounter with a work of art. But it's Simon Dinnerstein's fault. He beckoned. I hesitated. Then I followed. (He's pretty persistent.) I'm still trying to figure out who Simon is, what it was I was following and why I did it. But I'm not being coy. To begin with, there are two Simons. There's the elegant artist in his 70's whom I met a few years ago. And there's the young man in the blue velvet shirt, who's still staring out from his life in the 1970's, when both Simon Dinnersteins were young and in their 30's.

Both the painter and the painter painted appear in the monumental self-portrait, family portrait and—since its setting is a room and town and a time in Germany, a portrait that might be described with a not-quite-translatable word to convey its ambition—Simon Dinnerstein's *weltanschauung* portrait, called *The Fulbright Triptych*.

Weltanschauung? I know. It's one of those complicated, dressed-for-the-lecture-hall words the German language seems so pleased with itself to own and brag about. In English, we say, "worldview" but that's too weak and too vague for what the Simons were up to. To have a weltanschauung is really to describe a way of looking that attempts to place yourself in the cosmos, after a long, searching, philosophical examination of the whole phenomenon of human existence. Yes, all that. Which means, it's no wonder Simon Dinnerstein won't stop staring. There's a lot of responsibility in that look. (I mean the Simon Dinnerstein in the painting—though the living and breathing one is no slouch either in the philosophy department.)

I met both Simons the same day.

The beckoning of one and the other turned into the kind of afternoon of unrushed conversation—hitting it off with someone new—that can make you giddy and a bit forgetful of where and who you are when you finally have to get up to leave. And it was only my mid-aged self leaving the lobby of the German Consulate in New York. But, for a few hours, I listened and talked and looked back and forth at the two Simon Dinnersteins— artist and his painted, almost life-size self-image, four decades younger.

What was strange was how much the same they looked. I don't mean something out of *Dorian Gray*— the portrait hadn't aged; the person hadn't stood still. But I noticed two fascinating things. It seemed, for one, that Simon had painted himself forward into maturity. He's a new father in the painting, and he's a Fulbright scholar, after all, and there's that whole weltanschauung business. But—you'd think this might not be a revelation—I became aware of something else while looking from Simon to Simon. We get an unfair advantage in being alive. It was the charisma of Simon the painter moving, breathing and talking that made him seem almost as young as his silent, frozen, younger self. Our animation gives us an edge. It made me wonder if I should be more suspicious of portraits—or if maybe I should be more patient and give them, in their immobility, some slack.

To be really honest, part of me didn't want to like the portrait project of *The Fulbright Triptych*. "Like?" I know. But it was the State Department that had asked me to see it and to meet these Simons. I had a role as chairman of the Fulbright board under President Obama and I just assumed the artist and the painting had their roles too. I knew *The Fulbright Triptych* had been eloquently evangelized by a large chorus of the great and the good—artists and writers, art historians, critics, diplomats—all singing, "Masterpiece!" And I know the painting had been interpreted and explicated, provided with confident and scholarly taxonomies of references and allusions. Not that it was pop culture famous, but it seemed to be *known*—or, at least, pretty knowable. The *Triptych* didn't seem to be causing any trouble.

My instinct was, "Uh oh."

I agree that would not have been diplomatic. But I take artists seriously and I wanted to avoid being fumbling and fake. Even when it's meant, praise can box in both art and the audience. Reverence has a way of evaporating when somebody insists on it. We wander off, or love does, when we're not looking. And—I really believe this— when art is ignored, it can disappear.

The Fulbright Triptych was in no need of rescue. But I think I was. And that coincidence of me carrying around the loss of some kind of faith and then meeting and being deeply moved by the two Simons is something that's made me think long and hard about what art does and why we need it. I can describe what happened in two words: *blue velvet.* But I get nervous just putting things out there and leaving them alone. I'm more comfortable when things are complicated. And what if the right words were actually *blue velour*?

Let me explain.

All triptychs encourage storytelling. The three panels act as an unfolding of time, doors opening to deepening revelation. That's what happened the afternoon I met the two Simon Dinnersteins. The door opened, the Simons beckoned. I meet, first, a young wife and their baby girl in arms. Then, next, I'm standing both in and in front of a room with good windows and a good view of a small, sensible German town, laid out on a small, sensible German grid.

On the table in front of the window, the young Simon Dinnerstein has laid out on another grid the tools of his trade. His faith is visible. And he has pinned to the wall small drawings, quotations, postcards of famous paintings— evidence of his education and obligations, correspondence with himself and his friends and family, the living and the dead, citizens of his dreams.

The room feels open and capacious, but its objects—tools, furniture, spare décor—have real weight. They possess the gravity of metaphor and iconography. What we don't recognize, we think we should.

Then farthest to the right, young Simon sits in an open-collar blue velvet shirt. I wanted to ask the older Simon about that shirt. But the intimacy was a little unnerving. Why would it embarrass me to ask about clothes he'd obviously been comfortable enough wearing to paint himself in them for going on almost fifty years? But that brought up deeper questions, somehow even harder to ask questions, of all *The Fulbright Triptych* was trying to reveal and why.

When we follow strangers, hunches and unmarked roads, it's because something tells us—even in an age when we've pretty much abandoned the idea of forbidden knowledge—that we might discover more than we should know. It's irresistible danger, to risk that our worldviews might be upside down. But why do strangers trust us? Why do artists lay bare their lives and fears and dreams for us? We're strangers to them too. What kind of bravery is it—or curiosity, lust, chutzpah, maybe even moral propaganda for a way of life—that wants us to come in, look around, make assumptions, make as many claims on their lives as they could on ours?

I remember a scene from a documentary about Christopher Isherwood where the novelist is saying something particularly uninhibited about his past romances. His red-faced interviewer blurts out, "Why are you so honest?" Isherwood looks up and says, "Honesty is all I have." It's a wonderful answer, but I remember liking it all the more because there was probably a bit of an act to it. After Isherwood said, "Honesty is all I have," he waited a beat. Then he added, deliciously, "Honesty and a few adverbs."

If honesty is all any artist has, it really means, out of necessity, artists are exhibitionists. The etymology gives it away: *exhibere* means to *hold* something *out* in front of ourselves. Think exhibit, exhibition, exhibitionist. Then think portrait, science fair, courtroom, nudist colony, museum. But the etymology goes further: the root word *habere*—to hold—also gives us *habit*.

We make a habit of holding things out for others to look at: an object, a voice, a history, an attitude. Sometimes we hold out only our nakedness; sometimes it's only our shadow, eluding our grasp.

Our first habits were actually our clothes—everybody's clothes, not just the nuns. Clothes were what we held out on top of and in lieu of our bodies, exhibiting to strangers our occupations, our hometowns, our epistemologies, and how much or how little fear we had of our bodies. Eventually, the word "habit" came to mean our predictable behaviors—naked or not—because clothing offered such reliable shorthand for our histories, status and predilections.

It still does. Our worlds are defined by the parade of clothes, possessions and behaviors we inhabit and display—until we flee them. Our identities are beholden to our habits—until we shed them. But this way of putting it—shedding and fleeing—is itself a habit: in our time, we've become reflexively attracted to speed, ever-moving images, instability, shifts of gender, attention and geography.

But for almost half a century, Simon's blue velvet hasn't changed. It's there whenever I look for it—the open-collared seemingly casual shirt of a deeply serious artist. Looking at it over and over again—at the far end of the Triptych's story—has made me think that royal blue contained some clue about how to encounter, even to dwell in, a world governed - so differently from my own - by habits of stillness and calm, where, for however long its time needs to be frozen, nothing is shed and no one flees.

Habits of skepticism, habits of disenchantment and irony, habits that puncture praise and seek out dissatisfaction—my habits and the habits so common to contemporary art—die hard. But fortunately, even if they don't die, our hard certainties can lose their magic. What has been our faith and our comfortable habits can suddenly seem inadequate, no longer worthy of us, even unrecognizable and weird.

Weird and *worthy* actually have the same root in both English and German. Originally, to be *weird* was to have the power to control fate, to turn the world to our wishes. It is the fantasy of artists to be weird. To be *worthy*, on the other hand, was to have learned how to turn ourselves toward the world, to see things clearly and to face our fates, whatever they are. But is it anyone's fantasy to be worthy? We're so sure we already are. It may be one of the defining characteristics of contemporary life. In our boredom and narcissism, we've twisted desire into the impossible: we want the world to be worthy of us.

And, still, there is, and has been, young Simon in his blue velvet shirt, staring out of the canvas and into … what? The void? What did he and does he want? I didn't ask the Simon I was sitting with. It's the wrong thing to do and often deeply misleading to ask artists to explain their work. But I realized there was a clue in my interest in their silences.

The careful and learned organization of *The Fulbright Triptych* makes it easy to make the mistake that you can see this room, these three lives—man, woman, child—as a cabinet of curiosities. The German dictionary has a better word for that thing too, of course: a *wunderkammer*, a room of wonders. And you could think that's what we're supposed to be seeing—a room of the modest wonders and great ambitions of a young American artist abroad participating, with his wife and child, in an official government program of peace instead of being forced to fight, and possibly die, in the insanities of the Vietnam War, a war, in fact, that, just when *The Fulbright Triptych* was being painted, was forcing the end to the political career of the famous senator who fiercely opposed it and who gave the *Triptych* and the program for peace their names.

But I've come to believe this is the wrong way to read this great painting. It's not about the furniture of this artist's life or what's in his pockets. It's not some revelation about his passions or ambitions. It's not gossip or sexual attraction or politics or intellectual pride. All of these things are there, of course. They're arranged carefully for you to take note of them.

But the real secret and wonder, the real urgency of this stranger having beckoned you and me into this room, is that it's not a room at all. I don't mean that it's a painting, though of course, it is. What I mean is that what connects the act of its making almost half a century ago with the experience of uncertainty and shame and the eagerness so many people who've encountered it have to talk and ask questions and bring the family in it to life—what connects that frozen past to our present is that painting's joyful, mesmerizing exhibitionism freezes our time too. It causes an abeyance.

Abeyance means suspension. Maybe all great art offers that possibility, that feeling of floating, that we might be able to feel an uncanny pause in the unfolding of the next moment. I like to think a triptych offers a natural form for this feeling—three panels, as if to offer arms that can cradle us against its body and keep us from feeling the urgency of exit. It's what T.S. Eliot called "the still point of the turning world."

In the final panel of *The Fulbright Triptych*, Simon's shirt, the velvet and the blue somehow turn period and personality of the painting into something timeless. There is the blue sky of comfortable, suburban Germany outside the window. But over the body of the artist who painted his world of modest wonder, there is the rich, luxurious blue of deep space calling us in.

In Hebrew, Simon means "listen." I like to think it also means that the painter and the painter he's painted are exhibitionists of the needs of others—of our need to talk about and reveal ourselves. I like to think it means they intend their work to be more about us than them.

Tom Healy is an American poet and writer. Under President Obama, Healy served three terms as chairman of the J. William Fulbright Foreign Scholarship Board, which oversees the worldwide Fulbright Program.

4. Sonatina 1981

5. Renée 1970

6. Marie Bilderl 1971

7. Arnold 1972 *detail*

7. **Arnold** 1972

8. N's Kitchen 1970

9. The Sink 1974

10. Calling Card 1980 *above*

11. Joel's Shoes 1974-75 *right*

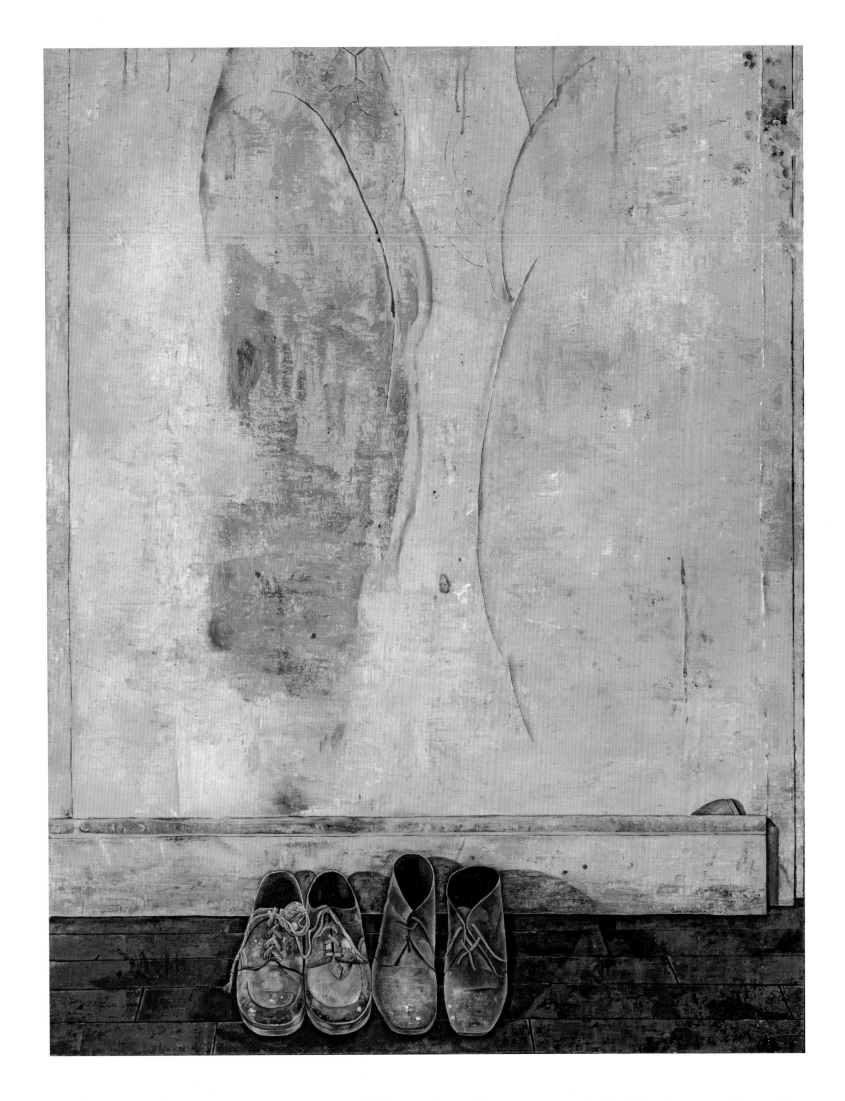

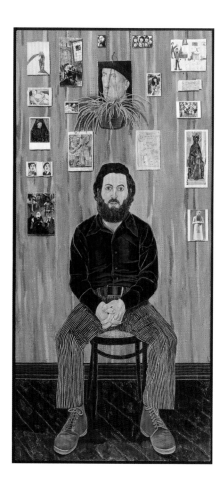

12. The Fulbright Triptych 1971-74
details follow

Simon Dinnerstein and Lynn F. Jacobs

The Fulbright Triptych

School of Law – University of Arkansas-Fayetteville, September 22, 2016

LJ I originally thought that this was going to be an interview, so I am going to start with questions. I am sure it will develop into a conversation. I would like to welcome you. Why don't you tell the story of the genesis of the triptych?

SD First I would like to dedicate this evening to two extremely good friends of mine, Miller and Jordan Williams, exceptional people.

I went to Germany on a grant in graphics. When I stopped going to art school at the Brooklyn Museum, I spent a few years drawing and doing prints. I had a friend, Shirley Pulido, who had lived in France for a year on a Fulbright Grant in fine arts. I was intrigued by the idea of living abroad. I remember speaking to Shirley about her experiences but didn't think my work was advanced enough to apply. To my surprise, Shirley told me that my art had progressed greatly and that I should seriously look into the Fulbright program.

I applied for a Fulbright Grant to go to Spain to study with Antonio López García who is an artist that I admire greatly. I got a letter back saying that my first choice didn't work out but that my second choice, going to Germany, did come through. The second choice was Germany to study the art of Dürer. Since art school, what I did was draw and do graphics. The drawings I do are quite large and extreme. I think that there are few artists working in the United States who take drawings this far.

It was difficult to find a place to live in Germany near the art school, which was located in Kassel. We finally located an apartment but basically I thought that it was not that interesting or inspiring. Everything in the apartment was very, very middle class and very cleaned up. Not a lot of atmosphere.

But, I drew. One of the drawings was of an old woman standing. About half way, or a little bit more than half way through the year, I found myself sitting at that table, engraving and looking out the windows. What is on the table are tools of engraving, so the plate is in the middle and you engrave the plate in a particular way, with burins. You cut the plate with burins. You basically turn the plate and drive the burins in a forward direction. Around the plate are burins, burnishers, scrapers. So, I was working in this manner.

For some reason or other, one day I moved back about 6 or 8 feet, looking at the windows and table and I thought that this view would make a terrific painting. I had been drawing, but I thought this should be a painting in color. Given the fact that I had spent all my time drawing, one could say that attempting a painting at this scale represented a tremendous leap of faith, but, nevertheless, I thought this could be a very interesting painting. The area that I actually observed was the table, the landscape and about half the pictures on the wall and half the objects on the table. I like putting up pictures. It's sort of like a refrigerator. You put up pictures and it defines who you are. The space for the people within my painting didn't really exist in the room I was working in. The room in my painting was becoming some sort of fantasy room, having begun life as a naturalistic one.

And then I got the idea that having people on either side would provide a different temperature in the wings than the middle. So the middle is slightly cooler and the exterior wings are slightly warmer. If you mingled those two temperatures together, you got a new temperature.

On the left side are images, pictures, reproductions connected with my wife and teaching. On the right side are images connected with art that had inspired me. When we came back from Germany in 1971, the middle panel was drawn in rapidograph pen. Every single line. This is quite compulsive. Every single line was drawn on a smooth white surface, which is composed of multiple layers of gesso. For the art students here, the wood panel is covered with many coats of gesso and then it is smoothed and sanded and the final coat you get something that is like ivory. I drew everything out in pen.

I started the painting in Brooklyn.

LJ It's a very large-scale painting. You didn't do any preliminary drawings, except for the engraving, right?

SD I don't recommend this. It is really, really nutty. There are no preliminary drawings. I just drew right onto the surface.

LJ Did you correct when you were doing that?

SD Some things were corrected but, basically, it was on point. But it means that the margin of error is very little or nothing. You're talking about .04 of one percent margin of error. I don't work like that now. I do studies and then re-work it larger…recompose it bigger. But this was done straight.

LJ But what was the reason that you had this painting on wood rather than canvas, which is obviously more commonly used by painters?

SD There is a difference between working on wood and canvas. It's hard for me to explain this. Wood seems to me more the medium of a draftsman. Andrew Wyeth's paintings are done on wood. Early Renaissance paintings—Flemish—are done on wood. George Tooker's art is done on wood. After the early Renaissance, and after the Flemish people, paintings got bigger. Wood at a certain size warps and moves around. If you actually look at the backs of Flemish paintings many of the backs have cradles on them. It's difficult. But the surface is very interesting. It's more anonymous. You can make textures with that surface.

Here's an example: the floor of the apartment we had in Germany was a standard parquet floor. When we got back we were really in bad shape financially and I put an ad in the local paper asking if anyone had a spare room. In return for the use of the spare room, I would do work for them and fix it up. Amazingly, someone responded. They had an extra room and it needed to be fixed up. The floor in the spare room was the support floor in a brownstone. That support floor is pine and then a fancier wood is put over it. Thus, the room had a support floor of pine that was painted a red color and that's the floor I painted in the triptych. It was really a lucky happenstance in that it was a lot better than the parquet floor, which had very little character. But that [support floor] had a lot of character! So the slatting in the floor was built up with gesso and thicker gesso almost like a relief. If you go up and look at the floor in the painting, you'll see it's thicker and has a place for the groove where the slots meet. You can't do that on a canvas. I needed a wood panel to do that. And then when I painted over it, the viewer's eye moves with the texture of the floor. You can have control with the use of the wood panel whereas the canvas—the texture of the canvas—it felt like it always controlled me.

LJ Well this is *The Fulbright Triptych* and you know I'm going to ask you this but why did you make a triptych? What does that format mean to you?

SD It's absolutely marvelous that I'm speaking with you. I first encountered Lynn's book visiting a bookshop at the Louvre Museum. In this bookshop—maybe it's because your book just came out—instead of your book being in the library position, it was facing front. I really loved it and made a point of remembering your name and thinking "this would be a great person to have a conversation with." I had seen a number of triptychs during the year in Germany and I think the triptych form seemed to me like a book. Elements in a triptych

converse with each other through space and in this case they converse middle to right; middle to left; wings to the middle; wings to the landscape. That conversation is very interesting and it's amplified by the separation. If an art historian was writing about this they would write all the reasons that this should be a triptych. It might be a little more than what I'm saying, but not much.

LJ I mean, what's been interesting to me about the triptychs that I've studied as an art historian is how the separations, the connections work within these parts. As you know, most of the Flemish triptychs are hinged and fold up. Did you think about doing it folding…or is it pragmatic? The scale of it would make it very hard to support those wings with hinges.

SD I didn't think of it folding but I did think of the three frames being bolted together. Each frame would then provide the visual space between each panel. The way it was eventually framed had to do with my gallery and how they wanted it to look.

There's another part of this that might be very interesting to mention…I worked on the painting for about a little more than a year. For the art students here you really have to be a little nutted out to devote yourself to creating art. I would like to think of this activity as *highly intelligent stupidity*. So I worked on this painting a little more than a year and we ran out of money—completely.…nothing. I had an idea of how I wanted to present my work. Many art students do a painting and then try to sell it. Students of mine have felt that. My idea was completely different. My idea was that I wanted to accumulate enough work to have a show that had a philosophy, that had a point of view. I don't quite know why, but that's what I felt. So we ran out of money and I remembered a gallery, Staempfli, that had shown Antonio López García. That show was the best show I'd seen of a contemporary artist. The reason his work is so good is that it's very figurative but it's also very modern and very pulsing with energy and haunting.

I was pushed against the wall and I didn't know what to do. So I took a bunch of photographs and went to that gallery—the first gallery I ever went to—and I walked in off the street. Now, for you art students, this is unbelievable. You just don't do this. I walked in and met Phillip Bruno, the co-director at Staempfli. This was on 77th and Madison Avenue. The co-director's role is to prevent you from meeting the gallery dealer. Like there's a moat and they're backing you away. So I told him that six or seven years before I had seen an exhibit of Antonio López García, was very struck by the work and felt that there was some connection between my work and his work. I asked him, "Would you take a look at these pictures?" For some reason, Phillip decided to look at them and that was extremely lucky. (I didn't realize *how* lucky it was at the time.) He looked at the photographs and said, "I'd like to show these pictures to George Staempfli." Soon after, they decided to come to visit me in Brooklyn.

Brooklyn *then* was not Brooklyn *now*. Brooklyn in 1973 was populated primarily by people born in Brooklyn. Where I live now in Brooklyn, we're two of the handful of people who were born in Brooklyn. I had the feeling that for this gallery Paris was closer to East 77th Street and Madison Avenue than it was to Brooklyn. So they came first to our apartment and then to this studio. They were tall, very distinguished and they stood in front of *The Fulbright Triptych* for a very long time. The middle panel was about two-thirds, maybe three-quarters done; the left panel was white; the right panel was white. I had given them a maquette of what was going to take place in each panel. They spent a lot of time looking at the painting—maybe 20, 25 minutes. They didn't say anything. Not a word. And then, George Staempfli, the owner of the gallery took out a very fancy cigar, a little black cigar. And he started smoking the cigar. And then, breaking the long silence, he said two sentences: "I think this a great painting and I'd like to own it." I almost fell on the floor. A few days later, I received a letter from George saying that they would like to buy the painting, *unfinished*, and pay every month for me to work on it. At the end of this time, I would have an exhibit there.

Just like in any fairy tale, there were two conditions to their offer. The first condition was that the painting had to fit into his gallery which was located on the second floor of an apartment building on the Upper East

Bar bara Ann

1 for   7 oth er

2 men   8 them

3 man   9 her

Side in New York. (To make a long story short, it fit; it got up there.) The second condition is pertinent to your question. The second condition was: "I warn you in *no uncertain terms* not to do the wings" Why? Because if you did the wings you would be making a painting that would be so large that no one could buy it. No museum could buy it. No collector could buy it. (And he couldn't sell it!) So here I was in this man's office. Very fancy. A big door was about to open. And so I—wacky enough—argued to do the wings. And I argued this way and that way and so forth and he was not convinced.

At the time I was reading a book by Hermann Hesse. The book is called *The Glass Bead Game (Magister Ludi)*. In this book Hesse describes the life of Joseph Knecht. After the story of Joseph Knecht is finished there is a section of Joseph Knecht's poems that were found posthumously; and then, after that, there is a section of essays and writings that were found after Joseph Knecht passed away. So I said to George Staempfli, "Why do you think that Hesse does this? He does it to flesh out who Joseph Knecht is; and these additional sections form the echo of his life." So George Staempfli, a very distinguished looking, sartorial man looked at me and said, "I knew Hermann Hesse." Wow!

So I bring this up because this picture was on exhibit for about three years at the German Consulate in New York. I have mentioned this story to other people. As much as I respected his opinion, I think that in this instance George Staempfli was mistaken. It seems to me that this is a much better painting with the wings. That's my opinion. Without the wings, it's a very good painting. It's very technically realized. But with the wings it has a left-right emotive force…and the human beings, too. But if I was smarter I would've said, "Yes sir, Mr. Staempfli, I'll do whatever you want, just give me an exhibit. Yes sir! " But I didn't.

LJ I'm glad it worked out. I love the story and I feel obliged to interpret your work for you.

SD But that's what an art historian should do!

LJ So I'm going to make an interpretation and see what you think of it. In this book that's been written about this triptych people are coming at it from many different viewpoints and I know you're open to many different viewpoints. I just wanted to throw my viewpoint in. So when I was thinking about this question—why wasn't it a folding triptych?—a lot of the triptychs I've studied are hinged and they fold and there's separate imagery on the outside. I started to wonder that maybe you put the outside of your triptych on the inside because you have two windows there and those windows have latches as if they could open up. So I was wondering how you feel about my interpretation that you have actually, in a certain sense, made a folding triptych because you have put the outside on the inside of your painting.

SD I like that a lot. I never heard of that before.

LJ (Laughing) Ah, very good! I think you may have subconsciously done that.

SD A man who was very helpful, really, genuinely helpful, in getting this painting here couldn't stay. He was just here at the beginning. His name is Don Judges and he is a professor here at the Law School and now works in a different area. The other night we were having dinner and I mentioned that it's very curious that an artist learns about his work *after* the artist does the work and, little by little, after and after and after…. And the artist isn't really special because most people do the same thing. They learn who they are "later." And then they'll say, "I learned this and I learned this." Then by the time they're 60 or 70 or 80 they'll say, "Oh, there's this theme that's running through." So, recently, on Facebook, I put a picture of a window on that I had done. Then I put another picture of a window. And then I put another picture of a window. And then another one. And I realized that I had 20 or 22 pictures of windows. And it never had occurred to me that windows were so important to me. And when I mentioned this the other day, Don Judges said, "Well, you have the windows in this painting." And then he said, "The whole thing is a window. It's a window into this world." I don't know…I kind of like that. I like that a lot.

Yours is great as well!

You should know that what Lynn is talking about is when triptychs close, they close to, usually, a grisaille—a grayish-toned image. So, for instance, *The Garden of Earthly Delights*—the wings don't open and close (at least, I've never seen that)—but, if it closed, you would see a grisaille of the earth. The creation of the earth, in the form of a globe, is depicted in gray. And when it opens you see everything in color. And the opening and closing related to, usually, religious holidays. I don't know what religion Bosch celebrated. That remains to be determined by you.

LJ That's a very long conversation that we probably can't get into today. But, maybe another time. So, in this book your daughter, Simone, said that you aren't interested in iconography; you're much more into some formal issues. Of course, I have to disagree with that—that obviously, one of the issues in this work that I hope that you'll agree with, is that this painting is about art. I wanted to ask you what you're saying here: is it a homage to art, to the artist, or both?

SD All of the above. The problem I have with iconography is that I spent some time at the American Academy in Rome. Iconography there was connected with—I can't remember the name of this theory about art…about interpreting art…it begins with an "S." Does anyone know the word?

LJ Semiology?

SD Yes! Semiology. And what I don't like about that personally is that it makes the art historian and the critic into, equal to, or greater than the artist. Now if I say that I don't entirely know what I'm doing and then, if I read a book and the art critic is writing semiology and they are saying "it's this, this, and this." I find that disturbing because they are saying "I think it's this…I think it's this…I think it's this, and, yes, this; this is what it is." On the other hand, iconography is symbolism which can be a kind of amorphic symbolism, playful. It can be in the air…it could be things that you don't understand. It could be lots of different things, but I think what Simone meant was more like semiology. So in this picture you have naturalistic details which could be symbolic. And you could make a good argument that the picture is about *process* and the creation of a work of art.

LJ Do you want to talk a little more about that? What do you mean by *process*? Where does it reside in the painting?

SD Well the *process* is located in the plate in the middle panel that is being engraved. Everything leads to that plate. That plate is like a sun…a wafer…a god. And all the pictures on the walls are the inspiration for what's going on in that plate. And when you do your art you have childhood influences…pictures that you liked as a child…you have your world as a child, your family, what your mother told you, your girlfriend, your boyfriend, the landscape you grew up in. All those influences and the pictures you respond to are the food that you're eating to create the art. You don't work out of nothing. And so my feeling is that all of these diverse images represent what I'm thinking… what's behind the artist. They're very disparate. There are a lot of children's drawings in here and I don't think you would see children's drawings depicted in oil paint prior to a hundred years ago. I don't think amongst paintings of the 16th, 17th, 18th, and 19th centuries you would see the depiction of a life of a child. Am I correct?

LJ Probably.

SD So the amalgamation of all these things is…*the artist*.

LK Your project that you got the Fulbright Grant for was to study the art of Dürer. But with so many images on the back of that wall, so many inspirations, there is no Dürer. So, where is the Dürer?

SD Dürer is the engraving.

LJ That's what I thought. Right answer!

SD There's one part of this that maybe you're not touching on. But when I got this grant I had hoped to go to Spain but I got it to go to Germany. This was 1970. Going to Germany in 1970 was very different than going to Germany in 2016. 1970 was just 25 years after the Second World War. We had very mixed thoughts about going. We had a definite pause about making this trip. And the idea that this painting came out of a year in Germany is flabbergastingly remarkable! It means that what you think is logical can always be overturned by… life. It means: don't be so sure about what you think is going to happen because I would have never thought of this painting coming out of a visit to Germany. And more than that, if I had gotten the grant to go to Spain, I would never have done anything as good as this.

LJ I'm asking you that because you are talking about the historical situation, it being 25 years after the war… also the '70s so we're dealing with the Vietnam War and in Germany it was a pretty tense time…the time of the Baader-Meinhof group and a lot of terrorism going on in Germany at the time. Were there any political issues that fed into this or was this deliberately stepping back into the aesthetic?

SD It was really the setting. I am not religious. I think I've gone to a synagogue four times in my life—two times by accident. But still you feel this extraordinary Second World War event. And we had many fascinating conversations. When this painting was on exhibit at the German Consulate, I would sometimes go down and hang out there. There was a write-up in *The New York Times* and it brought a lot of people there. One day there was an older couple who was there who were French. In their eighties. A very distinguished woman…wonderful looking! They were looking at the painting for a long time. So I came up and introduced myself and this woman said to me, "You see the flag on the outside of this building? I would never step foot in this building if it wasn't for your painting." It's so complex, life, that to find this in Germany, it's really unusual.

Now Dürer is what I would consider the prince of art. Dürer is German. He has all the characteristics of being German. But he is a prince. He is flying overhead. He is just amazing. He is one of the gods of art. And as I once joked about this painting, I remember saying that if Dürer was flying over Brooklyn and looking down at my painting, as he flew over he would smile and keep going.

LJ And write it in his diary. He wrote down a lot of stuff in his diary. One of the things in art history that we still talk about are gender issues. And there are obviously gender issues going on in this triptych. You have the left female side, the male side, the image of the women…and a male over you, the Van Eyck. Some people have commented that your wife and your daughter look like the Madonna and child. So, there are a couple of things I've been wondering. First of all, one of the standard things in the hierarchy of triptychs from the 15th century is that the left side or wing is for the more important and, normally, the male side. It's relating to the hierarchy from *The Last Judgement* because Christ's right side is his favored side (and, as a left-handed person, I'm not happy about that). But, nevertheless, that's the privileged side, that's the heraldic right side, and you've put your wife and your daughter in there and you've put yourself in the less hierarchically important side. Were you aware of this? Were you aware that you were doing this? Were you trying to play on the Madonna and child issue?

SD A little bit. As I mentioned earlier, this painting doesn't exist in real time. When I started the painting, my daughter wasn't born. And we didn't even think that she would be born. My wife was going to be holding that card with a "Y" on it. That card is a phonics card. And at that time, Renée taught a class of little children and she taught them to read by holding these cards up. (She hates this idea now.) But I liked the shape of the "Y." And the kids would sound out the four sounds of *Y*. Then my daughter came along—this was about a year and a half or so later—and I took the "Y" out and put my daughter in. I thought that my side was going to be too strong, so I thought that they would be better on the left side. The right side in Western art is stronger than the left. That's my hunch and I think I've read about this concept as well.

LJ Is that because we read from left to right?

SD I think it's because we read from left to right, and in Western art the right side is stronger and it's also true in theater. In theater, if you're looking at the stage of a theater, the right side is stronger. I felt that placing myself on the right was better. Since the right side was stronger, I was balancing the left side, which had two characters, Renée and Simone. I didn't think of anything more than that and I liked placing my daughter there, on the left.

LJ Just to get a little more general as we come to the end of our hour, I was wondering if you want to talk about – since you obviously have so many references to artworks of the past that inspired you there on the back wall with other kinds of things too—I thought it might be interesting for us to talk about what do you think the role of the art of the past is for the contemporary artist?

SD In the United States, critical thought would be that art began…about five years ago. And if you were a little less extreme, you would say, "No, it's not five years ago; it's about 20 years ago." And I think it's much more complicated and the problem that a figurative artist has is to deal with this tremendously long tradition that art has and to create something that is new or pulsing or modern or special…and to do it without a strategy…to do it out of your heart. And these other artists to me are inspiration and food for pushing that idea. I don't see how you could avoid that. One of the big knocks on figurative art is that the critic will say, "This is illustration" or "This is academic." And I think that's a very big mistake. I think that there really is something called "illustration" and there is something that is called "fine art." But when you call something that's fine art "illustration," it's pejorative. It's like you're doing this [*gestured giving it a "thumbs down"*]. And when you call something that's figurative, "academic," it's a loaded word; you're saying that [*thumbs down gesture*]. Do you agree?

LJ Oh yeah…that's definitely an issue for art today. There are a lot of people here today who are in our Foundation program and I was wondering what advice you might want to give to people who are beginning to think about possibly having a career as an artist?

SD I think the best advice I could give is "you only live once." I'm sorry to tell you, in my opinion, it's just one time around. If you think something else, you might be right but, from my point of view, it's one time. If you have a feeling about doing something, you should at least give it a shot. And give it a good enough shot to say, "I gave it my all; I tried; I did all that." You don't want to be the kind of person who gets to be 40 or 50 and says, "I should've done this; I should've tried." You really don't want that. So, that's my opinion but this picture took three years to do and you have to be quite worked up to do this one painting for three years.

LJ So can I ask you what your favorite triptych is and why, not including *The Fulbright Triptych* here?

SD Well if you consider the Van Eyck triptych of *The Adoration of the Lamb*, if you consider that a triptych, I would say that that's my favorite. And if you're learning about that painting in Lynn's class, that's a remarkable painting that was done in 1400-something and supposedly done by Van Eyck. It's thought that he is the inventor of oil painting. It's a very early painting and you could make a very good argument that painting has not advanced much more than that painting. If you consider the *Isenheim Altarpiece* by Grünewald in Colmar a triptych, I would put that on the same level. An altarpiece. It's a polyptych. So it opens a few times. There's also a painting in Beaune by Rogier van der Weyden that I think is a triptych. In many of the triptychs, the donors are painted into the painting. The donors are praying and they're in the painting. And in Beaune, Rogier van der Weyden has Chancellor Rolin praying and it's in a hospital, a converted hospital. This is very interesting. Chancellor Rolin, because of the religious background at the time, thought that if he built the hospital, commissioned the painting and got the artist to depict him praying, he would be in a select place in the next world. And regardless of what one thinks of that, it got the painting to be done. And the painting transcends whatever it was that he thought.

LJ So this triptych, *The Fulbright Triptych*, is from '70 - '74 and we're quite a ways out from when you painted this. I was wondering how you feel when you look at this painting and you confront your younger self—not so much physically, but how you confront your younger artistic self? How you feel when you look at that?

SD That's a great question. Really terrific. First off, I wish I had an inspiration like this again. That's one thing. I worked on this painting just about every day for three years, so I saw it all the time. More recently, I went down to the German Consulate maybe 75 times in the three years the painting was there. I've seen it many, many, many times. When I look at the painting, I cannot take it in. I can't put my arms around it. I can't grasp hold of it. It eludes me. And that is simply amazing because I know all the things in it. And I think that the secret of this painting is in the space between the pictures and the people and the windows and the table. It's that space between everything that's another theme in the painting. I just can't take it in.

LJ That's such an interesting answer because one of the things—we talked about the role of Dürer for you— one of the most interesting interpretations I've read about Dürer's *Melancholia* is that there is so much in this engraving that is deliberately designed to be something you can't grasp and, hence, it encourages a state of melancholia in the viewer because there is so much in there that it can't be grasped…

SD Terrific. That's terrific.

LJ So in a way Dürer is there in your painting.

SD I hope so. He's flying around overhead. I hope you look at his work—maybe it's a little out of fashion these days—but I think he's a total genius.

LJ So I think a good idea would be for us to end our conversation and go to look at the work.

SD Does anyone have any questions?

Audience Member Did you ever finish the engraving?

SD Yes, I did. There's going to be a traveling show, beginning next July, which will go to three venues. Not a lot of pictures, about 15. One of them is the print, *Angela's Garden*, and one of them is the actual copper plate for this work. Dürer engraved personally all those plates so the *Melancholia* that Lynn is talking about could have only been done by him. No one could have done that. Now, for instance, there were artists who engraved reproductions of paintings and those reproductions traveled around Europe. That's not the same as Dürer. All of his engravings were done by him. So yes, I finished the plate and I actually have done other engravings as well. One of these, *Polhemus Place*, will be in the traveling exhibit.

Audience Member What is the scale of *The Fulbright Triptych*?

SD It is fourteen feet wide by not quite seven feet high.

Audience Member What was your reasoning for the visual material on the wall behind Renée?

SD On my wife's side…the reading method that she taught had to do with phonics and had to do with circles. And the origin of the writing was based on circles and there's a fabulous picture next to the "Y" and that picture is a page of circles. When you go upstairs and look at this, the child who did this started beautifully…circle, circle, circle, circle, all neatly positioned on the line. Then the second line, same thing. And then the child started to lose it and the circles started to go like this [be drawn erratically]. And then the child really lost it and the circles [were drawn all over the place]. I loved the way the page looked because it was so sincere and earnest and serious and it was all about circles and I thought to include all that. You have to understand that this is not something that was depicted in so-called "high art." So a child's drawing, a child's art, is something that would be called "low art." It's like "primitive" or whatever. And I liked that idea. And what I thought was, can I get the oil paint to look like that? And, if you look at other parts of this area you'll see drawings, children's drawings, with crayons or pen or pencil. And besides the fact that they were wonderful-looking, my feeling was "can I get my oil paint to look like that?" And it was funny—very funny. And it was also not funny.

Audience Member Was it hard to part with it [*The Fulbright Triptych*] after you had made so many memories over the three years you worked on it

SD Yes. Very hard. You see the way Staempfli paid me the money, it felt like a deal with the devil. The guy was very imperious. He was playing around with me. He was offering me a future. And it was like—stories that have to do with a deal with the devil: We'll publish your book but you have to sign up with the devil. And I always thought that when the painting was finished and it went to him, he had a buyer for it and I would wheel it in and he would wheel it right out. But that wasn't the case. He did it. He just did it. And, actually, the gallery didn't have a huge amount of money. I was very surprised at what their resources were.

The other thing about this is that the effect of luck in life is not to be discounted. Staempfli was 64 years old when this happened. His wife, Barbara, was fabulously striking-looking. She was 32. And so, let's say he woke up in the morning the day he visited and he didn't have a good time with his wife the previous evening and was out of sorts. No way, Simon, no way. So luck is not to be discounted in life.

Audience Member Why is it in the law school?

SD It's in the law school for an interesting reason. It's in the law school because when it was on exhibit in New York it got a really wonderful response and a lot of people went to see it. There is an adage in American culture something like, "there are no second acts in American art." And, so this was like a second act for me. And I got very enthusiastic about wanting it to stay on view. And during the time it was on exhibit in New York, I met Stephen Reilly, the Executive Director of the Fulbright Association. I asked him, "is there someone connected with the Fulbright Program in a college, a university, or a foundation who would go for this idea." Stephen said he would like to help and he had on his board, Christopher Kelley, a Professor of Law at the University of Arkansas in Fayetteville. So he asked around and Christopher Kelley said he would like to help. I was introduced to Christopher and I thought, "Wonderful, great." And then Christopher introduced me to a man named Don Judges, who's not here now, and Don did all of the very, very hard work of getting the loan agreed to: humidity controls, fire codes, temperature, guards, lots of stuff. It really was exciting to me and I would like the painting to stay on view…because I felt that it was so exciting.

Audience Member Other thoughts about Fulbright and your painting being at the home of the Fulbright here? Was that word part of your title while you were there?

SD I thought the Fulbright Program was fantastic. I thought the idea of it was amazing. When you stay in a country for a year, it's not stereotypes any more. You really *see* people. And I think actually more Fulbrights would be better for the world. You really interact with people. I think it's a marvelous program and for you people who are in Fayetteville, during the Vietnamese War, Fulbright was one of three senators who opposed the war. That is a very hard thing to do. Another senator was a man named Wayne Morse from Oregon. We have in the United States a great feeling about individualism, but we also have a great feeling about conformity. It's a really great program and I think that *this* is the Fulbright Program frankly [pointing to *The Fulbright Triptych*].

Lynn F. Jacobs Distinguished Professor, Art History, the University of Arkansas-Fayetteville, is the author of *Opening Doors: The Early Netherlandish Triptych Reinterpreted.*

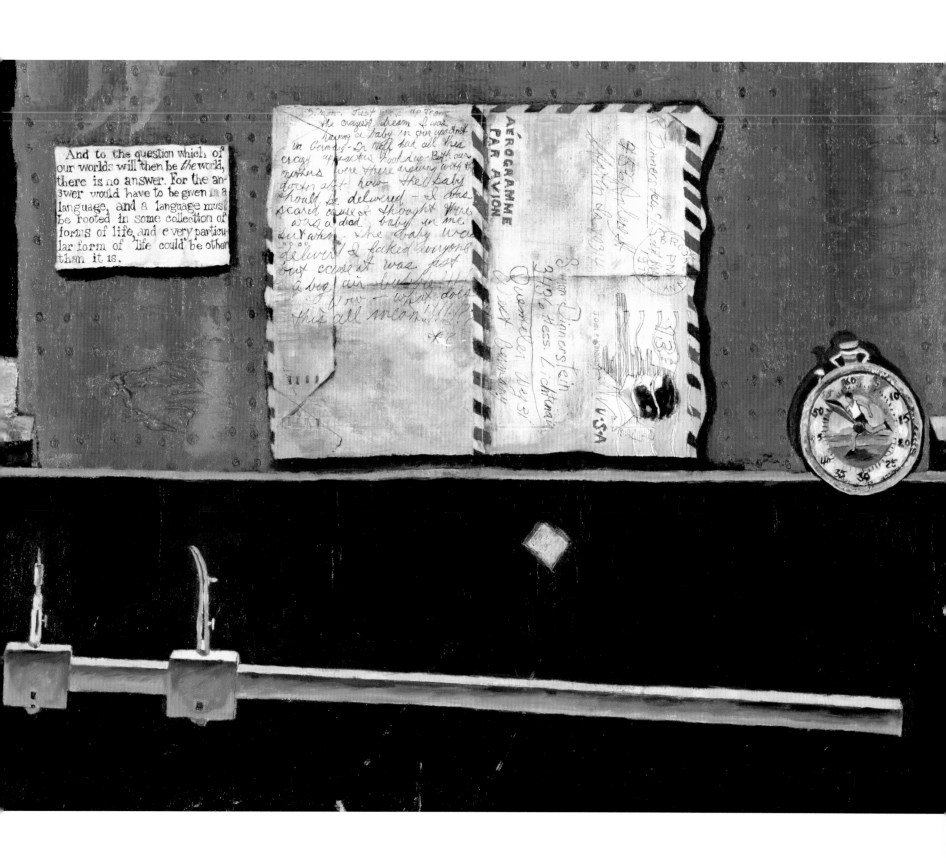

13. Night Scene I 1982

14. In Sleep 1983

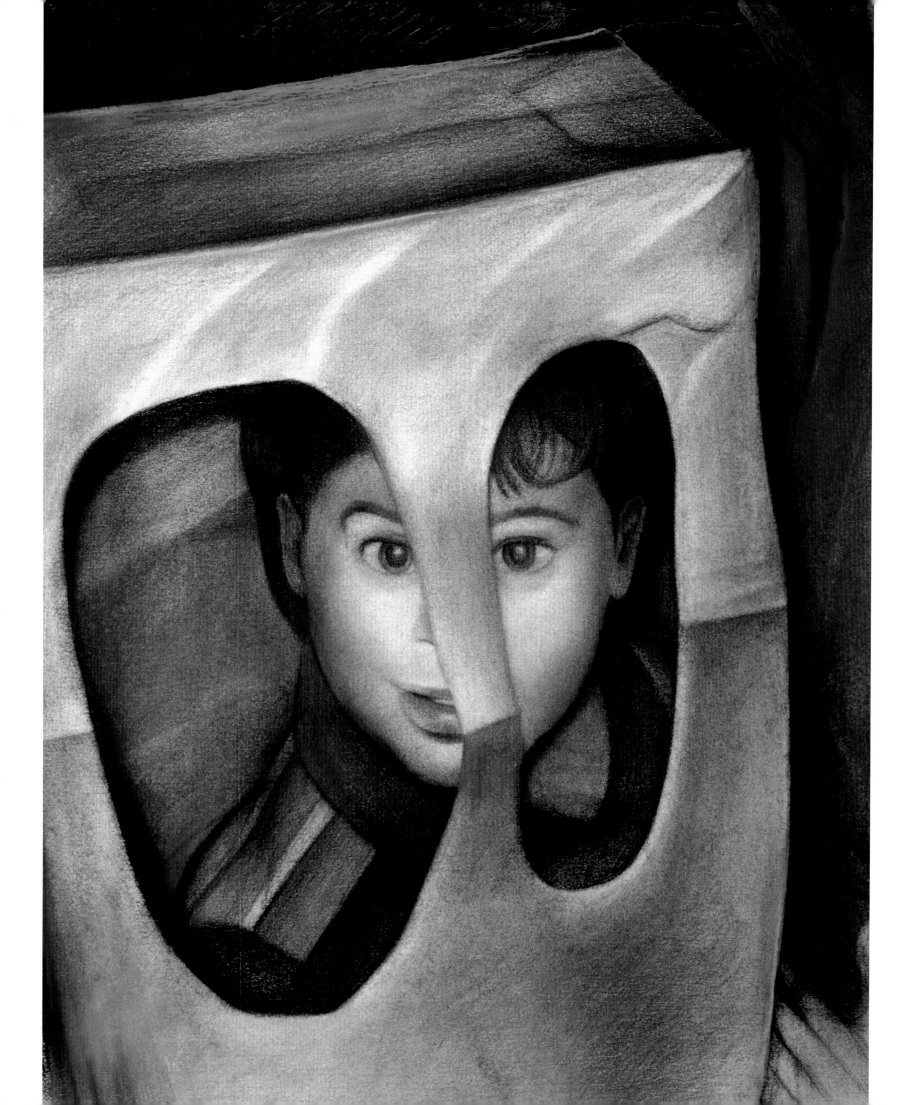

15. Night 1985

16. A Dream Play 1986

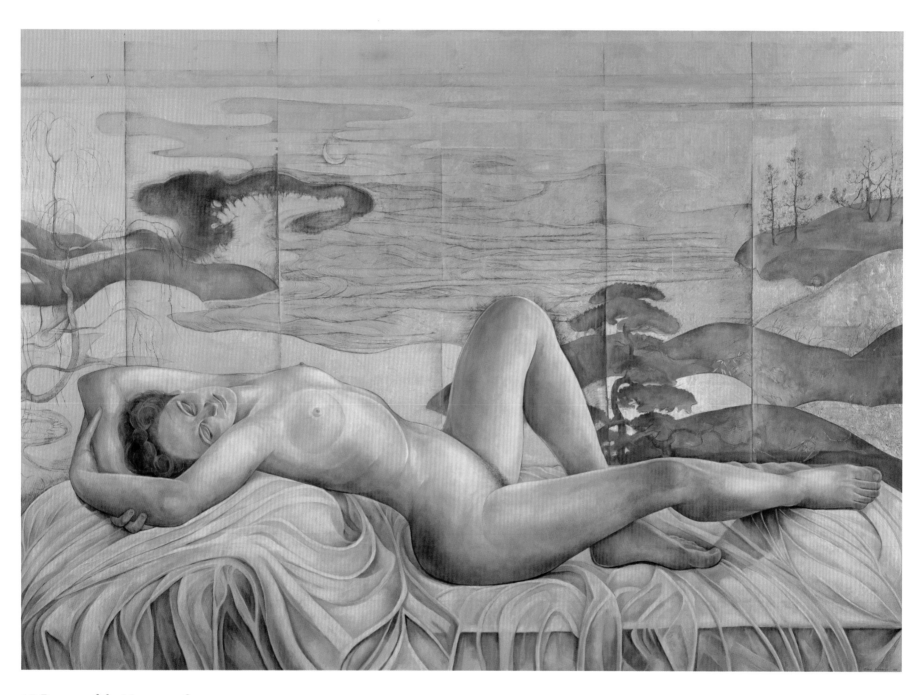

17. Passage of the Moon 1998

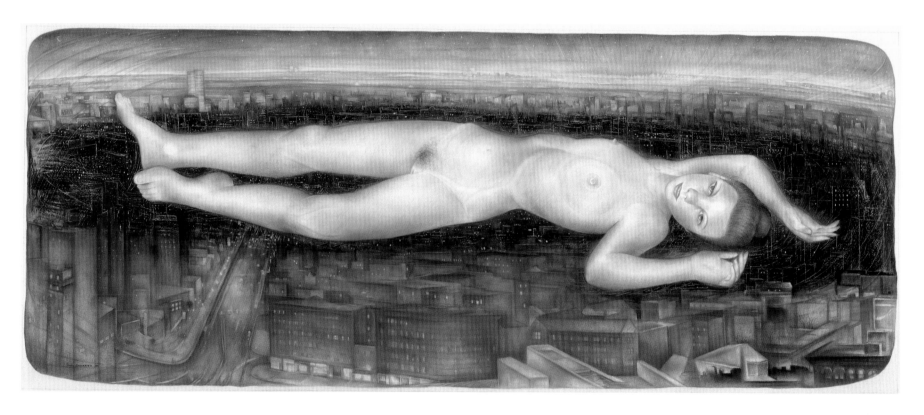

18. Purple Haze 1991

19. Polhemus Place 1969

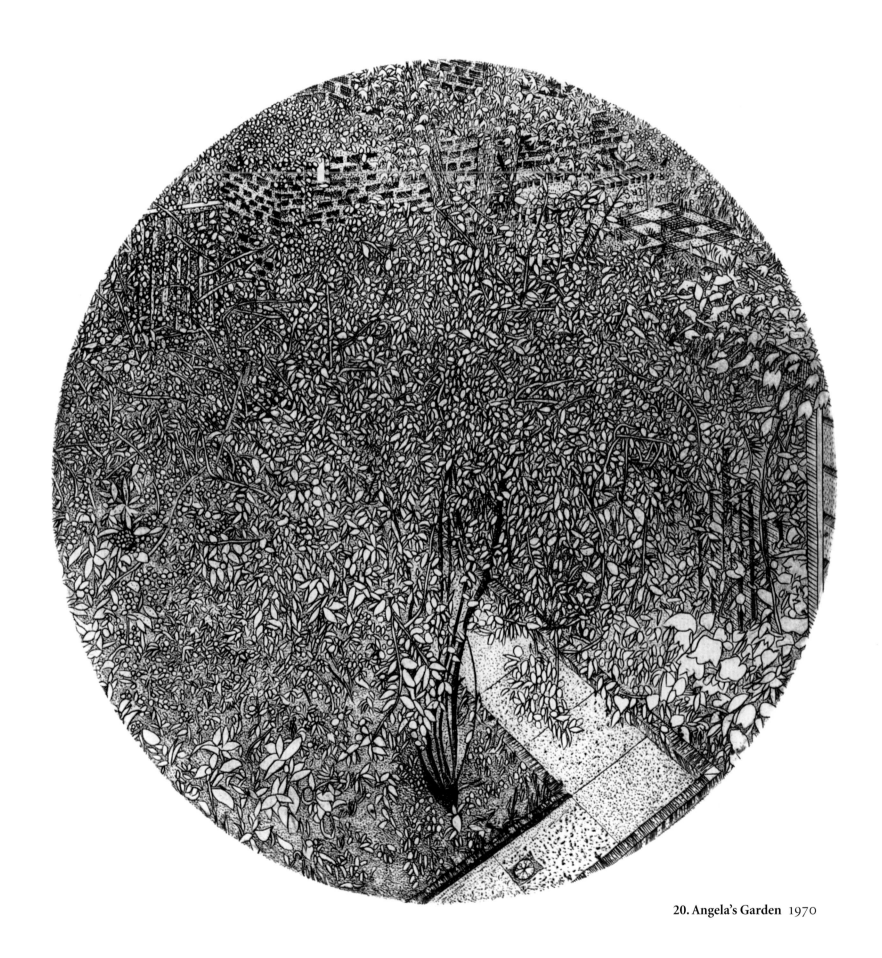

20. Angela's Garden 1970

21. Rear Window 1994

List of Plates

1. *The Fulbright Triptych,* 1971-1974
   Oil on wood panels
   14 feet in width, framed and separated
   Palmer Museum of Art, Pennsylvania State University, University
   Park, gift of the Friends of the Palmer Museum of Art,
   Pennsylvania State University

2. *The Kelton Press,* 1969*
   Charcoal, 25 1/2 x 39 1/2"
   Howard and Harriet Zuckerman, Monroe, New York

3. *Studio Still Life,* 1976*
   Oil on wood panel, 48 x 63"
   Munson-Williams-Proctor Arts Institute, Utica, New York
   Gift of the American Academy of Arts and Letters
   through the Childe Hassam Fund

4. *Sonatina,* 1981*
   Conté crayon, 26 1/2 x 40 1/2"
   Lucia and Brad Ginesin

5. *Renée,* 1970
   Charcoal, 25 x 39"
   Lawrence and Irene Lezak, Monroe, New York

6. *Marie Bilderl,* 1971
   Charcoal, conté crayon, 41 1/2 x 49 1/2"
   Minnesota Museum of American Art, Saint Paul

7. *Arnold,* 1972
   Charcoal, conté crayon, lithographic crayon, 84 x 36"
   National Academy Museum, New York
   Robert Dale Jones in loving memory of
   Mary Catherine Gray Jones

8. *N's Kitchen,* 1970
   Mixed media (silverpoint, gouache, tempera)
   and assemblage, 55 1/2 x 31 7/8"
   Dick and Maggie Dearnley, Little Rock, Arkansas

9. *The Sink,* 1974
   Oil on wood panel, 96 x 48"
   Museum of Art and Archaeology,
   University of Missouri-Columbia
   gift of the American Academy of Arts and Letters,
   through the Childe Hassam Fund

10. *Calling Card,* 1980*
    Oil on wood panel, 25 1/2 x 33 3/8"
    Estate of Lorraine Shatz, Montauk, New York

11. *Joel's Shoes,* 1974-1975*
    Oil on wood panel, 62 x 48"
    Dr. Jeanne Fenner and Peter Denny, Brooklyn, New York

12. *The Fulbright Triptych,* 1971-74 (See plate 1)

13. *Night Scene 1,* 1982
    Conté crayon, colored pencil, 41 1/4 x 29 1/4"
    Smithsonian American Art Museum, Washington, DC
    gift of the Sara Roby Foundation

14. *In Sleep,* 1983
    Conté crayon, colored pencil, pastel, 33 1/2 x 59 1/8"
    Smithsonian American Art Museum
    gift of the Sara Roby Foundation

15. *Night,* 1985
    Conté crayon, colored pencil, pastel, wax crayon, oil pastel
    36 1/2 x 76 3/8"
    Arnot Art Museum, Elmira, New York
    gift of Robert Dale Jones

16. *A Dream Play,* 1986
    Conté crayon, colored pencil, pastel, 38 1/4 x 82 1/2"

17. *Passage of the Moon,* 1998
    Oil and gold leaf on wood panel, 47 1/2 x 67 1/2"
    Henry Justin, New York

18. *Purple Haze,* 1991
    Conté crayon, colored pencil, pastel, wax crayon, oil pastel
    25 1/4 x 63 1/4"

19. *Polhemus Place,* 1969
    Burin engraving, 11 1/4 x 12 3/8"
    (Edition 125)

20. *Angela's Garden,* 1970
    Burin engraving, 11 3/4" diameter
    (Edition 125)

21. *Rear Window,* 1994*
    Pencil, powdered graphite, 75 3/8 x 40"

22. The artist with *Can the Universe be Held in
    the Gaze of a Small Dog,* 2011-2015*
    Pencil, powdered graphite, 69 7/8 x 84"

*Indicates reproductions of works not included in the exhibition.

22. The artist with *Can the Universe be Held in the Gaze of a Small Dog* 2011-2015

Biography

Simon Dinnerstein is an American figurative artist best known for his masterwork *The Fulbright Triptych.* In addition to 28 one-man exhibitions, Simon Dinnerstein is the recipient of a Fulbright Fellowship to Germany and a Rome Prize for study in Italy at the American Academy in Rome.

Born in Brownsville, Brooklyn, New York in 1943, Dinnerstein graduated from the City College of New York with a B.A. in History. Dinnerstein studied painting and drawing at the Brooklyn Museum Art School with Louis Grebenak, David Levine and Richard Mayhew.

Dinnerstein has exhibited widely. In addition to the present catalog, his work has been the subject of three books including, most recently, *The Suspension of Time* (Milkweed Editions, 2011), a 360-page publication dedicated to *The Fulbright Triptych.* This book is the only publication devoted to a single painting by a living American artist. Two monographs, *The Art of Simon Dinnerstein* (University of Arkansas Press, 1990) and Simon *Dinnerstein: Paintings and Drawings* (Hudson Hills Press, 2000), have been published on his work.

His numerous awards include a Louis Comfort Tiffany Grant, the Ingram Merrill Award for Painting, a New York State Foundation for the Arts Grant, and three Childe Hassam Purchase Awards from the American Academy of Arts and Letters. In 1999 and 2000, a retrospective of his work toured the country, sponsored, in part, by a grant from the Robert Lehman Foundation.

In 2017-2020, *The Lasting World*, an exhibit of Simon Dinnerstein's paintings and drawings, centering on *The Fulbright Triptych*, will travel to four venues. The highlights of this show are a symposium held at the University of Missouri-Columbia and the premiere performance of Robert Sirota's composition, *Three Nocturnes*, performed by Alarm Will Sound, based on three of Dinnerstein's works.

Mr. Dinnerstein, a member of the National Academy of Design, has been represented in past years by Staempfli Gallery and ACA Galleries in New York. He resides in Park Slope, Brooklyn, New York.

Chronology

1943   Born February 16 in Brownsville, Brooklyn, New York.

1963   Attends March on Washington, August 28.

1965   B.A., History, City College of New York.

1964-67 Studies painting and drawing on scholarship at the Brooklyn Museum Art School with Louis Grebenak, David Levine and Richard Mayhew. Becomes acquainted with the works of the American artists Edwin Dickinson, Gregory Gillespie and the French artist, Ingres.

1965   Marries Renée Sudler, August 28.

1967-72 Sees the films *Persona* (Ingmar Bergman), *Women in the Dunes* (Hiroshi Teshigahara) and *Solaris*, (Andrei Tarkovsky). Begins a life long interest in contemporary art films.

1968-69 Attends an exhibit of Antonio López García at Staempfli Gallery, New York. MacDowell Colony Fellowship.

1970-71 Studies on a Fulbright Grant (Graphics) in Germany. Resides in Hess. Lichtenau, near Kassel in north-central Germany and attends the Hochschule für Bildende Künste, Kassel. In 1971, begins work in Germany on *The Fulbright Triptych*. The painting (1971-1974) is completed in a Sunset Park, Brooklyn studio.

Travels to Nüremberg to see the exhibit commemorating the 500th anniversary of Albrecht Dürer's birth and to Ghent to view Van Eyck's *Ghent Altarpiece*. Visits Colmar, France to see Matthias Grünewald's *Isenheim Altarpiece*. Crosses the border to East Germany to see Dürer's original copper plate of *Philip Melanchthon* in Gotha, Germany.

Reads *Moby Dick*, completes reading book on the SS Rotterdam heading back to New York after a year's stay in Germany.

1972   Daughter, Simone is born September 18.

1973   In the midst of a personal financial crisis, approaches Staempfli Gallery *sans* invitation. George Staempfli and Phillip Bruno visit the artist's studio on Fourth Avenue in Brooklyn. George Staempfli purchases *The Fulbright Triptych* in its unfinished state and pays the artist monthly over the next two years to complete the painting.

1975   First one-man exhibition (Staempfli Gallery, New York).

Becomes a member of the faculty, New School for Social Research, Parsons School of Design, New York (through 2005).

1976-79 Lives in Italy on a Rome Prize Fellowship (Painting) to the American Academy in Rome (Lazarus Fellow, Metropolitan Museum of Art). Additional support is provided by grants from the Louis Comfort Tiffany Foundation (1976), the Ingram Merrill Foundation (1978-79), as well as two awards of support from the E.D. Foundation (1977 and 1978). One-man exhibit, American Academy in Rome, Italy.

Visits Paris and Vienna; views works of Piero della Francesca in Umbria and Tuscany. Encounters the poetry of Eugenio Montale. Meets the American poet Miller Williams at the American Academy and begins long-term friendship.

Three Childe Hassam Purchase Awards from the American Academy of Arts and Letters, 1976, 1977, 1978.

1979   One man exhibits: Staempfli Gallery, New York and the Institute of International Education, New York.

Lectures for United States Information Service (USIS) in Barcelona and Madrid, Spain. Meets Antonio López García in Madrid.

Adjunct lecturer, New York City Technical College (CUNY), Brooklyn, NY until 1988. MacDowell Colony Fellowship.

1980-81 One Man exhibit, New School, New York. Reads *The Brothers Karamazov* and *Crime and Punishment* (Fyodor Dostoyevsky).

1982-83 *The Fulbright Triptych* is purchased by the Palmer Museum of Art, Pennsylvania State University.

Work featured in *Hanging Loose* (*Simon Dinnerstein: A Portfolio*) edited by Robert Hershon.

Travels to Washington to visit the exhibit of Lucian Freud at the Hirshhorn Museum.

1983   Views exhibit of Frida Kahlo at the Grey Art Gallery, New York.

1984   Lectures at the Palmer Museum of Art, Pennsylvania State University, University Park.

1985   One-man exhibit, Gallery 1199, The Martin Luther King, Jr. Labor Center, New York.

1987   New York Foundation for the Arts Grant in Drawing; one man exhibit, Pratt Institute, Brooklyn (visiting artist).

1988   One-man exhibit, Staempfl Gallery, New York. Travels to Paris and London.

1988-89   Visiting artist, Calhoun School, New York, spring semesters.

1990   Publication of *The Art of Simon Dinnerstein* by the University of Arkansas Press (with essays by Albert Boime and Thomas M. Messer, epigraph by George Tooker). Begins a 15 year correspondence with Guy Davenport. Continues long term series of paintings and drawings of the nude.

1991   Travels to London. Completes the drawing, *Purple Haze*. Subsequently, at the suggestion of a Russian friend, Eugene Neifach, reads *The Master and Margarita* (Mikhail Bulgakov).

One man exhibit, St. Paul's School, Concord, New Hampshire. Visits the artist George Tooker in Hartland, Vermont.

1992   Elected member, National Academy of Design, New York.

1993   Travels to Madrid and Toledo. Visits retrospective exhibit of Antonio López García at the Reina Sofía Museum in Madrid. One-man exhibit, New School for Social Research, New York.

Simone Dinnerstein is married to Jeremy Greensmith. The artist gains a son-in-law and, moreover, a dear friend.

1994   *An American in Rome* at the Visual Arts Center of New Jersey, Summit, New Jersey, a large-scale exhibition of four recipients of the Rome Prize.

1995-96   *Collection Update*, National Academy of Design, New York, exhibition of acquisitions to the collection. Panelist, MacDowell Colony Symposium, moderated by Brendan Gill, National Academy of Design, New York.

1995   Travels to Mexico to see the work of Frida Kahlo and the murals of Rivera, Orozco and Siqueiros. Views Rivera's murals at the School of Agriculture in Chapingo. Visits Frida Kahlo's Blue House (*La Casa Azul*) in Coyoacán and the collection of Dolores Olmedo in Xochimilco. Travels to Rome and visits Orvieto to view the Luca Signorelli murals in the San Brizio Chapel.

1996   Travels to London to see retrospective of Alberto Giacometti at the Royal Academy. Returns to Italy for six weeks to revisit Rome, Florence, Padua and Venice. Views exhibit *Japan in Italy* at the Palazzo delle Esposizioni in Rome.

1997   Begins teaching classes in drawing and painting in his Park Slope, Brooklyn studio.

Representation by ACA Galleries, New York and Munich (1997-2006). Appears in group exhibitions at ACA Galleries in New York and with exhibitions of ACA Galleries at the Basel Art Fair in Switzerland and Carol Craven Fine Arts in Martha's Vineyard, MA.

1998-99   Work featured in *Ontario Review* (*The Art of Simon Dinnerstein: A Retrospective*), edited by Joyce Carol Oates and Raymond Smith.

1999-00   One-man exhibition, ACA Galleries.

The drawing, *Arnold*, is included in the exhibition, *Men Without Women: Paul Cadmus as Curator*, National Academy of Design, NY

Publication of *Simon Dinnerstein: Paintings and Drawings*, Hudson Hills Press, (essays by Rudolf Arnheim, Guy Davenport, Robert L. McGrath, John Russell, Edward J. Sullivan, Miller Williams).

The retrospective travels to: Bread and Roses Gallery, Local 1199, New York; Saint Peter's Church, New York; ACA Galleries, New York; Walton Arts Center, Fayetteville, Arkansas; Texarkana Regional Arts and Humanities Council, Texarkana, Texas/Arkansas; Marsh Art Gallery, University of Richmond, Virginia.

2001   Grandson, Adrian Greensmith, son of Simone Dinnerstein and Jeremy Greensmith, born on December 23.

2002   Begins series, *Palette Paintings*. Travels to London to see Lucian Freud retrospective at the Tate Britain.

2003   Travels to Vienna to view Dürer retrospective at the Albertina.

2005   Gabriela Lena Frank, commissioned by Astral Artistic Services, Philadelphia, composes *Ghosts in the Dream Machine* based on Simon Dinnerstein's drawings *Sonatina, Nocturne, Night Scene I* and *Night Scene II*. Composition performed by the Chiara String Quartet and pianist Simone Dinnerstein at Queens College, New York; Trinity Center for the Performing Arts, Philadelphia; and at the Appalachian Summer Festival, Boone, North Carolina. Subsequently performed by Ursula Oppens and the Cassatt Quartet in 2011 at Symphony Space, New York.

Travels to Madrid for the exhibition, *The Spanish Portrait*, at the Prado Museum and to London to see an exhibition of Frida Kahlo at the Tate Modern.

2006-07   *At the Still Point*, (72 x 79") a major painting in the palette paintings series is completed. Hosts an Open Studio to present this painting along with other works in the palette painting series.

2007   Travels to Amsterdam to see exhibit *Max Beckmann: Exile in Amsterdam*, at the Van Gogh Museum and Helene Schjerfbeck exhibit at the Gemeentemuseum, The Hague. Visits Bruges and Ghent. Ends journey in Paris and views exhibition of Anselm Kiefer at the Grand Palais.

Simone Dinnerstein's recording of the *Goldberg Variations* is released to great response and fanfare.

2009-16   Multiple Open Studio exhibits at Brooklyn studio; participates in the Annual Exhibits at the National Academy; Exhibit of giclée prints at Loupe Digital in New York (2010).

2012   Begins teaching *Art and Visual Perception*, a seminar in art appreciation in his studio.

Travels to Vienna to view Egon Schiele exhibit at the Leopold Museum.

2011-14   Publication of *The Suspension of Time*, a book devoted to reflections on *The Fulbright Triptych* by 45 writers, including Jhumpa Lahiri, Anthony Doerr, George Crumb, Edward Sullivan, John Russell, Rudolf Arnheim, Thomas M. Messer, Guy Davenport, John Turturro, Robert Beaser, Daniel Epstein, Colin Eisler, Philippe Grimbert, with an interview by Marshall Price. The publication is the only book devoted to a single painting of a living American artist. *The Suspension of Time* is selected for *Barnes and Noble's Year's Best Reading 2011: Editors Picks*.

Exhibit of *The Fulbright Triptych* at the German Consulate (2011-2014).

Cousin Corinne's Reminder, Issue Number Three, is published, Zack Zook, Executive Editor. It contains Jhumpa Lahiri's essay on *The Fulbright Triptych*, *The Space Between the Pictures*, with 24 details of the painting.

Robin Quivers moderates an on-stage conversation at the German Consulate between Simon Dinnerstein and Simone Dinnerstein.

Artist Ann Tracy moderates a conversation at BookCourt, Brooklyn between Simon Dinnerstein and Jhumpa Lahiri.

2014   Spends a month in Paris and visits Beaune to see Rogier van der Weyden's *Beaune Altarpiece* and returns to Colmar to see Matthias Grünewald's *Isenheim Altarpiece*.

The Fulbright Triptych is exhibited at the University of Arkansas-Fayetteville, School of Law (2014-2017)

2011-15   Major drawing, *Can the Universe be Held in the Gaze of a Small Dog*, (69 7/8 x 84") is completed.

2015   Spends a month in Rome and Italy. Visits American Academy in Rome, Naples, Pompeii, Orvieto (Signorelli), Venice, Padua, Florence.

2016   Visits Rome to see an exhibit of Balthus and to Paris to view the Anselm Kiefer exhibit at the Beaubourg Museum and at the Bibliotheque Nationale de France.

Daughter, Simone Dinnerstein performs the *Goldberg Variations* at the Opera Garnier in Paris with the Paris Opera Ballet.

Renée Dinnerstein's book, *Choice Time: How to Deepen Learning Through Inquiry and Play* is published by Heinemann. The book, a meditation on education for the young child, stressing curiosity and exploration, represents a fifty year career in education.

A conversation at the University of Arkansas-Fayetteville Law School with the noted art historian, Lynn F. Jacobs (author of *Opening Doors: The Early Netherlandish Triptych Reinterpreted)*.

2017-19   Traveling exhibit of 15 works with *The Fulbright Triptych* as centerpiece, is organized by Alex Barker, Director of the Museum of Art and Archaeology, the University of Missouri. It travels to: Museum of Art and Archaeology, University of Missouri, Columbia; Arnot Art Museum, Elmira, New York; Nevada Art Museum, Reno, Nevada.

A catalog for the exhibit is published with essays by Alex Barker, museum director; Rudolf Arnheim, psychologist; Tom Healy, former Chairman, Fulbright Scholarship Board, 2012-2014; and interview with Lynn F. Jacobs.

Alarm Will Sound, a contemporary chamber ensemble commissions Robert Sirota to compose, *Three Nocturnes*, based on three works of Simon Dinnerstein, *Night*, *Night Scene 1*, *Purple Haze*, for a premiere on July 27, 2017. The performance accompanies the exhibit at the University of Missouri, Columbia.

Ellis Ludwig-Leone is commissioned by the Terezin Music Foundation to compose a work based on the art of Simon Dinnerstein which will be performed by Simone Dinnerstein on October 8, 2018.

A symposium on *The Fulbright Triptych* takes place on September 22-23, 2017 at the University of Missouri, Columbia. Begins work on *At Four*, a reflection on the theme and voyage of childhood (80 1/4 x 83").

The Fulbright Triptych is exhibited at the Visual Arts Center of New Jersey, Summit in the Spring, 2019.

Selected Bibliography

Publications

"The Suspension of Time: Reflections on Simon Dinnerstein and *The Fulbright Triptych*," (360 pages, *Milkweed Editions*, 2011)

"Simon Dinnerstein: Paintings and Drawings" (128 pages, *Hudson Hills Press*, 1999)

"The Art of Simon Dinnerstein" (270 pages, *University of Arkansas Press*, 1990)

Videos and Podcasts

"Simone Dinnerstein and Simon Dinnerstein in Conversation: An Interview with Robin Quivers" at the Consulate General of Germany, *Vimeo*, 2011

"Triptych: An Evening of Painting and Music" (Simon Dinnerstein, *The Fulbright Triptych* and Robert Sirota's, "Triptych," performed by the Chiara String Quartet), *Vimeo*, 2014

"Simon Dinnerstein and Lynn F. Jacobs, In Conversation: The Fulbright Triptych," University of Arkansas-Fayetteville, Law School, *Vimeo*, September 22, 2016

Kyle Kellams: "Masterpiece on UA Campus," KUAF Interview, University of Arkansas-Fayetteville, September, 2016

"Exhibit at the Tenri Gallery, New York: A Walk Through with Francis Cunningham," 2011

"Simon Dinnerstein and *The Fulbright Triptych*," interview with James McElhinney, *Newington-Cropsey Cultural Studies Center*, April, 2013

"Simon Dinnerstein–Meet the Artist," *Smithsonian American Art Museum*, Interview, May 15, 2015

Ann Landi, "Grounded in the Figure, Interview with Simon Dinnerstein," *Vasari 21*, October, 2016

Articles and Reviews

Roberta Smith, Senior Art Critic, *The New York Times*, "Rediscovered at the Altar of Art," August 11, 2011

Roberta Smith, Senior Art Critic, *The New York Times*, "Simon Dinnerstein: The Fulbright Triptych," Museum & Gallery Listings, September, 2011, the listing appears for 100 weeks during the 3 year duration of this exhibit (2011-2014)

John Russell, Senior Art Critic, *The New York Times*, "In Dinnerstein's Painting, an Echo Chamber," February 5, 1975

Thomas M. Messer, "No One Could Accuse" *The Suspension of Time, Milkweed Editions*, 2011, Daniel Slager, editor

Jhumpa Lahiri, "The Space Between the Pictures," *Cousin Corinne's Reminder*, Issue Number 3, an essay on *The Fulbright Triptych*, with 24 color reproductions of the painting and details.

Donald Kuspit, Contributing Editor, "Simon Dinnerstein: German Consulate General," *Art Forum*, November, 2011

James Panero, Managing Editor, *The New Criterion*, "Exhibition Note," September, 2011

Peter Trippi, *Editor-in-Chief*, "Savoring Simon Dinnerstein's Fulbright Triptych," *Fine Art Connoisseur*, Jan/Feb 2014

David Cohen, Introduction to "The Art of Simon Dinnerstein," by Guy Davenport, *Art Critical*, October 7, 2011

Daniel Maidman, "Simon Dinnerstein's Irregular Grid," *Huffington Post*, February 13, 2014

Tim Nicholas, "Simon Dinnerstein: Analog of a World," *Painters' Table*, March, 2014

Jonathan Liu, "Simon Dinnerstein Says: Lethem, Lahiri, Turturro and Others Write a Painter's Gospel," *New York Observer*, May 31, 2011

Kaitlin Pomerantz, "Luck of the Paint," *BOMBLOG*, August 30, 2012, *Bomb Magazine–Artists in Conversation*

Jhumpa Lahiri, "The Space Between the Pictures," *The Suspension of Time, Milkweed Editions,* 2011, Daniel Slager, editor

Anthony Doerr, "You are the Printmaker," *The Suspension of Time, Milkweed Editions,* 2011, Daniel Slager, editor

Rudolf Arnheim, "Pictures of the Lasting World," *Simon Dinnerstein: Paintings and Drawings, Hudson Hills Press,* 2000

Guy Davenport, "An Exchange of Letters," *The Suspension of Time, Milkweed Editions,* 2011, Daniel Slager, editor

Edward Sullivan, "The Theology of Art," *The Suspension of Time, Milkweed Editions,* 2011, Daniel Slager, editor

Edward Sullivan, "The Urban View in the Art of Simon Dinnerstein," *Simon Dinnerstein: Paintings and Drawings, Hudson Hills Press,* 2000

Albert Boime, "Simon Dinnerstein's Family Romance," *The Art of Simon Dinnerstein, The University of Arkansas Press,* 1990

Jon Kalish, "When Simpsons' Co-Creator Sam Simon Pulled Out of a Portrait Commission, Simon Dinnerstein Made a Few Changes," *Art News, April 1, 2015*

Sarah Douglas, "Retrospective: At the Guggenheim's Memorial for Director Thomas M. Messer" *New York Observer,* September 17, 2013

Austin Williams, "Inside Artists' Sketchbooks," *Drawing Magazine,* Summer, 2016

"Featuring: Simon Dinnerstein," *Colored Pencil Magazine,* December 2014

Aubrey Godwin, "Life Becomes Art in a Visual Memoir of the Fulbright Experience" *Fulbright Review,* University of Arkansas, Fayetteville, Summer, 2014

Elana Hagler, "Pursuing Humanity: An Interview with Simon Dinnerstein," *Painting Perceptions,* April 21, 2013

Eric Herschthal, "The Jewish Echoes in 'The Fulbright Triptych' " *The Jewish Week,* August 9, 2011

Rebecca Park, "The Fulbright Triptych: Portrait of the Young Man as an Artist," *Diplomatic Courier,* 2012

Hirsh Sawhney, "Fiction Chronicle," *The New York Times Book Review,* reproduces a detail of *The Fulbright Triptych,* July 3, 2011

Elissa Schappell, Hot Type, *Vanity Fair,* July 2011, reviews *The Suspension of Time*

Publisher's Weekly, "The Suspension of Time: Reflections on Simon Dinnerstein and The Fulbright Triptych," June, 2011

Cynthia Maris Dantzic, "100 New York Painters," *Schiffer Publishing Ltd.,* (November 2006)

Gabriela Lena Frank, "Ghosts in the Dream Machine for Piano Quintet," *(Composer's Statement),* March 14, 2005

Ilana Abramovitch, "From Brownsville to Park Slope: An Interview with Simon Dinnerstein," *Jews of Brooklyn, Brandeis University Press;* 1st edition (November 1, 2001)

Deborah McLeod, "From Visceral Portraits to Romanticized Nymphs, Bodies of Work," *Richmond Times,* September 1, 2000

Roy Proctor, "Exploring the Edge: No Slave to Fashion, Artist Draws us into Other States of Mind," *Richmond Times-Dispatch,* August 20, 2000

Joe Maniscalco, "An Artist at Work: Park Slope Painter Lets You in on the Creative Process," *Park Slope Courier,* January 31, 2000

Richard Mertens, "Essential Realities: Simon Dinnerstein Draws the Essence of Art from the Commonplace," *The Concord Monitor,* October 25, 1991

Theodore Wolff, "The Kind Word for Such Art is 'Conservative' " *The Christian Science Monitor,* April 25, 1988

Simon Dinnerstein, "Looking At One's Own Artwork" *American Artist,* April, 1986

Doug Turetsky, "Simon Dinnerstein: Artist in the Round," *Brooklyn Affairs,* April, 1985

Bennett Schiff, "On a Roman Hill Scholars Dwell in an Estate Of Mind," *Smithsonian,* March, 1978

Michael André, "Simon Dinnerstein (Staempfli)," *Art News,* March, 1975

John Gruen, "On Art: Freilicher, Fish, Dinnerstein, Peterson, Baber," *The SoHo Weekly News,* February 6, 1975

George Staempfli, "Simon Dinnerstein," catalog essay, one-man exhibit, *Staempfli Gallery,* January 14 - February 8, 1975

Acknowledgments

The Lasting World had the privilege of being curated by Alex Barker, Director of the Museum of Art and Archaeology, University of Missouri. His idea for a symposium on *The Fulbright Triptych* creatively connects Alex's curiosity with a sense of the dialogue within the arts and humanities. A traveling show is like a very complex and large jigsaw puzzle and Alex worked wonders at putting all of the pieces together.

Thanks should be given to a number of individuals that contributed towards the catalog: Frances Babb; Dr. John D. Babb; Eric Brecher; Liza Bruna and Sam Zygmuntowicz; Cynthia Curne; Isaac Erlich; Roberta Feldman; the Fulbright Association, Washington; Mary Gannett; Lucia and Brad Ginesin; Marsha Gray; Dr. Susanne Grennell; Doug Hecklinger and Kyle Kimball; Jason Kaplan; Nicholas King and Rachel Spear; Rita Knox and Enos Donawald; Larry and Irene Lezak; Loupe Digital, New York (Michael Tolani and Chris Daciuk); Ragnar Naess and David Charles; Robin Quivers; James Rosenfield; the Lois Roth Endowment, Washington; Jacqui Rubin and Matthew Healey, in memory of Lee and Barth Healey; Peter Scotese; Mickey Swee; Howard and Harriet Zuckerman. In addition, I have great appreciation for Peter Scotese's significant contribution toward the exhibit.

A great deal of gratitude goes out to the lenders to the exhibit: the Smithsonian American Art Museum, Washington; National Academy Museum, New York; the Minnesota Museum of American Art, Saint Paul; the Palmer Museum of Art, University Park; Pennsylvania: Arnot Art Museum, Elmira, New York and the Museum of Art and Architecture, University of Missouri, Columbia. Special appreciation to the private collectors who lent to the exhibition: Dick and Maggie Dearnley; Henry Justin and Lawrence and Irene Lezak. I would like to acknowledge the efforts of David Walker, Director, Nevada Museum of Art, Reno and the museum's curator, JoAnne Northrup, and to Rick Pirozzolo, Director of the Arnot Art Museum, Elmira, New York and curator, Laura Wetmore.

Thank you to James Senzer at Loupe Digital for developing the color and imaging for the catalog. Michael Tolani and Chris Daciuk at Loupe have worked over many years to produce high quality images of my art.

Thanks to the photographers Peter A. Juley and Son, Bruce C. Jones, Studio/Nine Inc., Eric Pollitzer, Jeff Wilcox, Steven Tucker, and Adam Reich, whose fine work forms the basis of these reproductions.

Thanks to Lev Mendes for his fine and inspired copyediting. My appreciation to Todd Bradway for his insightful suggestions. Peter Nevraumont and John Coughlan contributed helpful advice.

My daughter Simone, her husband Jeremy Greensmith, and their son Adrian, contributed great advice and understanding.

The catalog is dedicated to Renée, whose presence means the world to me and whose love made all of this possible. How lucky I am!

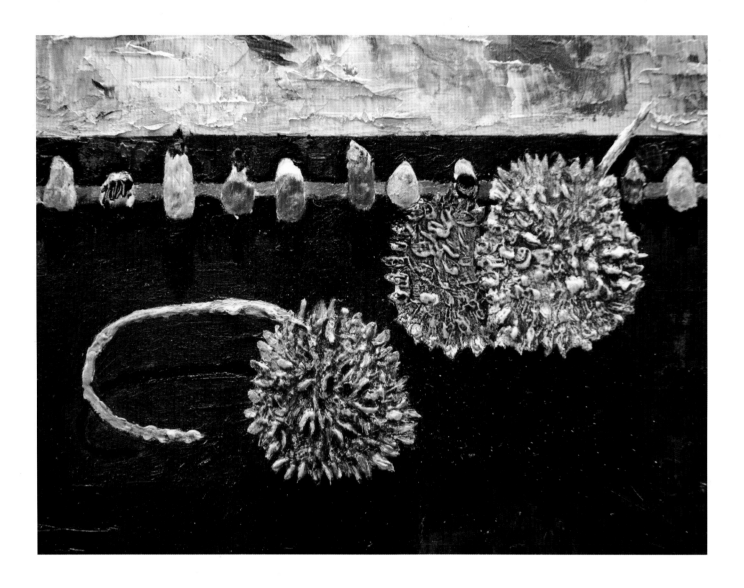

"It is striking, and also fitting, that a novel so distinctly American, a novel about appearance and reality, about Ishmael's reflective wandering and Ahab's ruthless quest, informs the creation of the Triptych. For this is a painting, among other things, about what it means to be an artist: a necessary combination of Ishmael's absorption of the world, fused with Ahab's ruthless passion. It is also an intensely personal painting, just as *Moby Dick*, for all its vastness, is an intensely personal narrative. It is a painting about a young American artist's absorption of Northern European art, about his study of Dürer's copper engravings, about his response to that discipline in a new medium, and about his journey home. The triptych-in-progress not only crossed the Atlantic physically along with its creator, but embodies dense layers of crossings between one thing and another: between artistic traditions, between places, between past and present, between the real and the recreated. Between emerging and being, and between conception and birth."

— Jhumpa Lahiri author, *Interpreter of Maladies*